... *ready, steady,* ....

Go. See. Do.

10 life Changing Quotes to be successful as a young professional

www.mjvonline.com

GO. SEE. DO.
Copyright © 2018 Go. See. Do., LLC
ISBN 978-1-54394-292-7

Designed by Kaitlynn Jolley
Illustrations by Annalina Väth

Fuel the passion for life with Author Maika Janat for giveaways, updates, and great advice at http://www.mjvonline.com.

Go. See. Do.

10 LIFE-CHANGING QUOTES
TO BE SUCCESSFUL AS A YOUNG PROFESSIONAL

Maika Jauat

To my daughters
Marlene & Lucy

**Wherever life will take you,
I hope this book may be a great guide for you and
empower and inspire you to**

Go. See. Do.

Contents

PRAISE FOR MAIKA JANAT

"It was an honor and true pleasure to see Maika evolve as a person and a leader throughout her journey in our company. I will never forget the energy and her determination at her first interview with us, applying for a job as an apprentice. She kept that energy alive and stayed true to herself throughout her entire high-speed development from apprentice, junior, project manager to managing director. Maika was able to capture some of that in her book to hopefully inspire others."
-**Nico Ubenauf**, *Founder and CEO, satis&fy*

"In a world where it's easy to assume career growth can be as complicated as a chess game, Maika shows us our best ladder is good, common sense. She succeeded when it seemed unlikely by living and breathing her Go. See. Do. attitude."
-**Jessica Roy**, *Global Process Innovation, Nike*

"This is a book for everyone eager to be extraordinary, like Maika. A career does not come on a silver platter with benefits and a great work-life-balance on the side. But anyone can have one, and Maika's recipe is compellingly simple: follow your inner compass, and with the right attitude, dedication, and hard work you can move moun-

tains. And this is something not only young professionals should read."
-**Fee Vogel,** *Founder and CEO of vitaminfee GmbH*

"While reading Go. See. Do. I found no surprises, because the words fully reflect her leadership style. She is the real deal. The tips and advice she gives are based on her approach to building a team and business, and while working for Maika I witnessed the success."
-**Patrick Tyvand,** *Director of Operations NA, satis&fy LLC*

"Maika is a passionate business woman and has always managed to pursue her personal dreams and goals alongside her professional career. She has been a great mentor to a lot of young professionals. I wish her all the best for her future adventures as a professional and daring woman."
-**Nancy Schacht,** *Global Director of Project Management, satis&fy*

"Honest, practical, and heartfelt is what makes this a must-keep-close-and-break-in-case-of-emergency personal navigation handbook. It will help all, not just to navigate a professional career, but, more importantly, to become a better person."
-**Eitan Wynalda,** *Creative Director, Lev Creations*

If there is one person in the world I would always trust to get things done and done right it is Maika Janat. She is the ultimate professional with only one level—her absolute best! She is also kind, generous and a pleasure to work with. Her book is full of powerful little gems that, if followed, can really make a positive difference in anyone's career!

-Tona' Broussard-Wilson
Executive Director & CEO, Now&Zen Productions

"Maika has an incredibly authentic approach to business and represents what modern leadership is truly about. These insightful stories from her journey provide an incredibly inspiring backdrop for anyone starting out or feeling lost in their career!"

-James Montague, *Nike, General Manager Football, UK/ Ireland*

"This book is so eye-opening, authentic, and inspiring — I want to read it over and over again. Maika is a great role model, and I am lucky I got to work with her. Her story is so magical, and it will be motivating to so many people, both young and older, from all over the world. This book is truly a gift for all people that are out there and want to go and get it!"

-Sophie Matlé, *Project Management, satis&fy, LLC*

FOREWORD

You may not be an event planner. You may not even know what goes into planning an event. That doesn't matter. Life is an event, or a series of them, so allowing you into the world of an event planner will tell you all you need to know about how to handle life, or at least the business elements of life.

At this point, I'll tell you about event planning so when you read Maika Janat's stories you will better understand her points of reference. And, if you are already in the world of event planning, skip the next paragraph and go directly to the one after it.

Event planning is defined as third on Forbes' list of most stressful jobs. It is entirely about creativity, strategy, and detail. Let's give you an extreme example in case, so far, you've been planning sorority pool parties or cousin's wedding showers. Let's say that Steve Jobs (yes, we know ... let's assume this was in the past) wants to announce the next new Apple product and says, "Arrange it." You, as the event planner need to dig deep and find out what it is, why it's being introduced, to what audience and how many of them, understand that product in great detail, find the perfect venue, arrange for a worldwide broadcast, get people invited, then registered, sometimes transported from all over the world, provide food and beverage, often with 38 different dietary requirements, arrange airport pickups, find furniture that suits the brand, design audio visual and appropriate content, and the list goes on. That's what is known as planning an event. Now Opening Ceremony of the Olympics is also an event, so take that into consideration. With all of that in mind, meet Maika Janat.

Maika is my friend and colleague. She has generously written a "how to" book filled with advice for those entering the business world, though her stories could also influence those of you who have been doing business for years, but maybe not as successfully as you'd like. Maika is a go-getter, an enthusiastic, smart, and savvy young woman who seized opportunity fearlessly, dove off the high dive of business, and emerged successfully with integrity, authority, and ingenuity. She began as an intern to a German event production company in 2004 and since then rose in the ranks to become President of their U.S. operations. Her chapters will tell you her story.

I asked her why she wrote this book, and she told me that she wished that a book like this had existed when she started in the business. She's right. In ten chapters you will get advice on how to succeed, and you will be motivated and encouraged in the best of ways.

So, read and enjoy her journey, because she's a very special lady. If you follow in her footsteps you will be wiser for it.

-**Andrea Michaels**, *Founder and President*
Extraordinary Events

I wish i would have
had this book

PREFACE

I have learned much over the last 15 years working in the live events industry. My experience has shaped me. I began as an intern and became the president of the first North American branch of an international company based in Germany. I am writing this book for the next generation.

If you are either starting a new job, thinking about taking the next step in life, or wondering why it appears everybody else is moving forward except you, *this book is for you*. If I had been able to read a book like this 15 years ago, my life would have been much easier. I am sharing what nobody else ever shared with me.

the Secret of getting
ahead is
    getting startet

INTRODUCTION

Whenever I am asked how I managed to create a successful career starting at the age of 18, I recall a famous quote of Mark Twain:

> *" The secret of getting ahead is getting started. "*

Very true, but how do you really get ahead of the game?

Begin anywhere.
Get started.
Take action.
Stop talking and start doing.

This is literally what I did in 2004 when I began my career in the event industry. I had no idea what my end goal would be and where life would take me. But I had stopped thinking about it and started doing.

While all my friends were still going to college to prep themselves for a job in the real business world, I already had one and was learning through experience. I had managed to get myself an apprenticeship as an event manager at a well-known global event production company.

The life lessons I experienced were real; I could feel them mentally and physically. Rather than a class I took in school, I lived each moment, good and bad, and learned from each of them.   I was able to make an impact on a project from day one because I worked in the real world and contributed to a corporation and the global economy as an adult citizen.

I can't think of a better teacher than the event industry when it comes to a well-rounded education. Planning and executing an event is the best executive training for a young professional to learn the good and bad techniques of leadership. Documenting the pros and cons of an event, including lessons learned, is a key task to making the next one even more successful for everyone involved.

Based on my 14 years of work experience, I have filtered out 10 quotes to live by as a young professional. Each one contains an element that will lead to success.

I share them with you in this book. You define the rules on how to read this book, and you decide how to use these quotes in your daily life. I just want you to get started so you can get ahead!

Are you ready?
Go. See. Do.

listen to your heart

ONE

listen to your heart

I share a lot of good advice with you in this book, but the most important is to listen to your heart. To be successful, you need to base your decisions on what your gut and heart tell you. There is no better source of excellence and passion from which to pull.

When I graduated from high school, my teachers recommended I study medicine or law because of my stellar grades. My parents would have loved to have a doctor in our family, but they knew me and proposed I major in journalism or sport management.

As I talked with others about my future, the possibilities expanded. However, I was unsure of what I really wanted. The opportunities as well as the social pressure and expectations overwhelmed me. Realizing that I needed to simplify the process, I created my own formula:

BE SUCCESSFUL =
MAKE THE RIGHT DECISION

MAKE THE RIGHT DECISION =
BE GOOD AT MAKING THE RIGHT DECISION

BE GOOD AT MAKING THE RIGHT DECISION =
LOVE MAKING THE RIGHT DECISION

LOVE MAKING THE RIGHT DECISION =
KNOW WHAT THE RIGHT DECISION IS.

KNOW WHAT THE RIGHT DECISION IS =
LISTEN TO YOUR HEART

Ways to Listen to Your Heart

As simple as it sounds to listen to your heart, it is the most difficult step to take in this process. But once completed, the next steps will be easier. I promise. The best part is you don't need anyone else to help you do it. Start right here. Right now:

- Find a happy place or action. It can be your favorite spot in your house, a bar, a coffee shop, a park or an activity like running, biking, or cooking. You know best what makes you happy and where your brain has time to reflect, think, and listen to your heart.
- Be honest with yourself. This is just about what you want, not about what you should do.
- Think about five things you love doing.

- Decide on five activities in which you have talent.
- What you love doing and are good at doing can be anything and doesn't have to be related to any business or industry yet.
- Write down the five things you love and the five activities at which you have some talent.
- Words like *maybe, probably,* and *eventually* do not exist when you listen to yourself.

To give you an example, these are the notes I wrote down for myself:

Organizing Parties
Travelling
Sports
Making Plans
Working in a Team

   As soon as you have landed on five things, start considering businesses, industries, and job profiles that fit those skills and strengths. Knowing them will enable you to sell yourself with confidence. It eliminates faking anything. With that skill set and confidence, no one can ignore you. Remember the quote, "Love what you do, and you'll never work another day in your life." That's what makes you "real" to others. These factors make you differ from all the others around you and will automatically lead to a successful career start.

You will be surprised how many matches you will find and how obvious what you should do becomes.

Build a Story Around Your Skills and Use It

Does this require extreme intelligence? No. Does it mean you have to excel in at least ten skills? No. Does it mean you need to speak fifteen languages or have travelled the world before high school graduation? Absolutely not. Focus on the things YOU are good at and build YOUR STORY around them. That's more than enough to get started.

- Once you find a job profile for which you know you are a perfect fit, do research on the actual jobs in that industry.
- The moment you find an open job position that fits your skills, apply for it. Include your story and why you want that specific job. Explain how this job embraces what you love in your application letter.
- Create an application letter design that you like that fits your story. It will differ from all other letters and will pop out.

You will find out that no matter if it is your application letter, the first interview, or introducing yourself to colleagues at work or to clients, you have your story. You can tell why you took this job and never have to make something up. You will never feel you have to explain or justify yourself, because you are real. This strategy allows you to just be you. Based on that you can make the right decisions, and that will make you successful.

This is the path I followed to begin my career in the event industry and how I found the company where I worked for fourteen years.

listen to your heart - What's your story?

make it

OR

break it

TWO

Make it or break it.

The one way to be successful when you start a new job:
MAKE IT OR BREAK IT.

Here is why:

I finished high school and managed to get myself an
exciting apprenticeship at a well-known production company. I had a defined goal: I wanted to be a successful
event manager and be rewarded for all my decisions and
effort getting to this point.

However, the reality was that I had a job in a new
industry about which I knew nothing and needed to learn
from scratch. I was far away from a career as a successful event manager.

I once learned at a TEDx talk in Portland that "En-
titlement is stinky cologne." And that's so true. A career
doesn't just happen. A dream job isn't waiting for you. You
must make it happen.

I was 18 years old and one of many girls who wanted to be in events. Competition was big, and my dream jobs were rare.

Every Moment Is Valuable for Your Career

Not all of the tasks were sexy. I made coffee for others and was in charge of writing the minutes for every meeting. It sounds totally cliché, but honestly — what do you expect when starting your first job after school?

"You have to be conscious of the fact that every task you're getting will be useful and will lead to your ultimate goal. It's all in your perspective," my mentor once told me, "and this job has to be your priority." She was right.

Despite what is taught in school, learn to be self-taught. Reflect upon new skills to be able to use them again. Working doesn't allow re-reading a chapter again to gain more practice.

I discovered the easiest way to learn was to show interest in every single detail about the company and its projects. I always volunteered for any and everything whether it was assisting with a project or overseeing the phone at the front desk. My colleagues would consistently teach me, but I learned it was better to be a self-starter and figure it out on the go.

Everything took me longer. but I always went the extra mile and did not count my hours, I did not calculate my hourly salary, and I moved my vacation if there was a new job popping up. I did not compare my job with the gigs my friends had gotten in other industries. I focused on myself, my company, and my tasks.

As time passed, I became involved in so many aspects of the company that my associates started coming to me asking the most random questions because they felt I knew the answers. And guess what? I knew. I could tell them the secret spot for spare keys, how to do specific expense reports, or train the new cleaning staff on the coffee machine in the warehouse. No problem.

The more experienced I became, the more I could do. This sparked creativity within me. I could give colleagues and clients a variety of options, depending on their needs. This, in turn, caused everyone to depend upon me for their needs. This increased my productivity for the company.

It's All About Priorities

I became so busy that my family and friends started giving me a guilt trip every time I had to cancel plans with them. Nine out of ten times when I tried to go for a drink or see a movie with a friend on a work night, I ended up cancelling at the last minute. My dedication drove me to working up to the time I should leave and realizing I needed to stay and finish my work. I started hearing, "You work too much! You are not the boss of the company yet! They are taking advantage of you! It's just a job! Think about your priorities!"

Whenever that happened, I would remember my mantra — make it or break it.

I counted my blessings. I got to travel; I had great colleagues; and I had discovered something that I really enjoyed doing. I was very happy with my first real job, and I tried everything to make my colleagues and bosses happy so that I could stay on forever.

Others who had started their jobs at the same time as I did tried to talk me into saying NO at work. They thought if we would all say NO to our leadership teams they would comply and adjust our schedules and salaries accordingly.

My response to them? If you are the client and your project manager tells you: "Sorry, this is too much work, and we want more money," would you hire them again? Or, if you were the boss and your team constantly told you that they had private commitments and other excuses why they couldn't take responsibility for the job, would you promote them or even retain them? Finally, I summarized with, "It's not on us to decide when we have worked enough. Our job is done when it's done."

It wasn't easy, and sometimes I felt disloyal to my

young colleagues. But through it all, I kept my mind on my goal of being a successful event manager.

It's the same during set-up of an event. You can never go to a client when you are onsite and say: "We haven't completed the job, but we have worked twelve hours today and think it's enough. We think we deserve a break and will go home to have some fun now. Unfortunately, your event is not ready to go yet." They would for sure never hire us again.

No matter what your future goals, be fearless. Be assured that you need to focus on your goal and take responsibility of your tasks without compromise.

MAKE IT OR BREAK IT.

THREE

Now or never.

NOW or NEVER situations are game-changing. Game Changers lead into successful careers.

My game changer occurred on a Friday night as I was ready to leave the office based in Berlin, Germany. My boss called and told me the company planned to set up an office in Portland, Oregon, and they wanted me to do it.

After we hung up, I Googled "game-changing." Just to double-check, I researched it on Wikipedia. This is what I found: "Critical and having the potential to alter the overall outcome."

Ways to Learn if It Is a Game Changer Situation

I compared my situation to this explanation and came up with a quick five-step game-changing reality check list:

1. A game-changer is a now or never decision.
2. You are the only one who has been asked to do this
3. You are the first one to get this chance to make it successful.
4. This is a business opportunity that is also a personal opportunity.
5. A game-changer is very challenging at first.

Based on this five-point check list, it will take less than five minutes to know if you are in a "Now or Never" game-changing situation.

If you can answer at least three points with a YES, you should take the next step: ACCEPT IT.

The Power of Positivity
Why should you always say YES to a NOW or NEVER decision?

- This particular opportunity will never occur again.
- You have nothing to lose. This is not the end of your life.
- The secret of getting ahead is getting started.
- The older you get, the less flexible you become.
- It will never be easier to do it than now.

- You learn more than you would in any other situation.

These five points are reasonable, and they are even easier to accomplish if you think them through:

- You have been gifted with this one chance. They want you, nobody else, to do it. So, they trust you and want to support you. Why would they pick someone they thought wouldn't be successful? You need to have your boss's back!

- Change is the only constant. You are not making the last decision of your life. This is about a job and living in a city. This is not about having a baby. You can always change it again.

- In a game-changing situation, you start from scratch. You don't take over from another person. You start on a blank piece of paper. You have the freedom to create it the way you want.

- It won't get easier the older you get. Your personal situation might change, but you may not be up to life-changing challenges as you grow older. This is your time now!

- It will never be easier, the expectations of

you will never be lower, and you can be at your best. You will save tons of time and energy thinking about "what would have happened" if you don't do it.

- You will learn so much more in a new situation: You will learn about your new job, your new life, your new world, and about yourself. You will be able to add to your story, your experience that nobody can ever change again.

No matter which kind of game changer it is, don't be afraid. Fear is your worst enemy.

So, whenever you get a lifetime opportunity: Take it. Don't overthink it. Sometimes it's just NOW or NEVER, and that's okay.

By the way, six months after this phone call, I found myself in Portland, Oregon, launching an office. I'm thrilled I took this one-time opportunity that changed my life.

be so
GOOD
they can't ignore you

FOUR

Be so good they can't ignore you

Many very talented young professionals, like you, are vying for fewer, really cool jobs. To ensure you get to do what you love and love what you do, be so good they can't ignore you.

When I was asked to set up an office in Portland, Oregon, I didn't have a lot of aces in my back pocket. I did not know the city, I did not know the competition, I did not know how to do business in the U.S., and I did not have a lot of clients. Too many negatives, right? I knew and respected the many well-established event agencies in town. I wasn't sure if there would be a place for me and my business when I moved from Germany.

Upon our arrival in Portland, my associate, Michael, asked, "How do we make sure we are so good they can't ignore us? "We had to hit the ground running from day one.

What It Means to Be Good

I told him the lesson I learned from former German soccer player and current U.S. national soccer coach, Jürgen Klinsmann. He once said in an interview: "You don't have to be the best to win the world championship; you just have to be three percent better than the average!

Way back when I was a teenager, this mindset was eye-opening to me. I realized there are other ways to become the best in class and be successful rather than studying for years, having a lot of experience, and being highly intelligent.

I started focusing on the three percent that I needed to be better than the average and came up with the following 10-point mix of social skills and work attitudes:

BE KIND
RESPECT EVERYBODY
BE ACCOUNTABLE
NEVER TAKE IT FOR GRANTED
BE RELIABLE
TAKE RESPONSIBILITY
BE REAL
KNOW YOUR SHIT
BE LOYAL
WORK HARD

Always stick with these points. They don't come in a certain order.

It doesn't matter if it is your first day at work. if it is a small or a big task you get asked to do, or if you are just having a conversation with a colleague. Michael and I lived by these 10 points, and they were the keys to our success.

They sound simple, but what do they really mean and how can they be transferred to your daily work?

Simply put, they mean:

- Have a smile on your face when you walk into a room, a location, a restaurant or when you talk to somebody. Even when it is over the phone.

- Let people finish their sentences and tell their idea and their plan without judging it right away. Respect that they have a different opinion than you or have their own way of doing things apart from you.

- Do what you say you will do. If you told a client you would send an email the same night, then better send it the same night. Even if it isn't needed that early.

- Serve people. Guide people into their comfort zone and pick them up when they are down. Show empathy for what their challenges are.

- Follow up and be proactive. Don't wait for your boss or your client to come back to you.

- Be proud of any task you can do. Never think anything is too small or too big. Never judge and never feel entitled.

- Be open to new things and be positive, even if you don't like the task you have been given.

- Re-read an email before you send it. Have a colleague cross-read a quote or a presentation to make it better. Four eyes always see more than two eyes.

- Google your clients to learn more about them. Pay attention when they order a coffee so that you know how they like it and can bring them one next time.

- Ask for help if you need it. Say stop if you can't do it.

- Come prepared. Go through the questions you want to ask before the meeting. Write them down for reference.

- Finish a task from A-Z and think the topic through further. Go the extra mile.

- Be honest when you make a mistake. Apologize without finding any excuses.

- Do things correctly and as best as you can.

- Remember, more work in the beginning means less hustle in the end.

It sounds like a lot, but it doesn't have to be done all at the same time. Not all of it must be done.

It's the attention to the details on all levels that will make you so good they can't ignore you.

the only way
to have a friend
IS to BE one

FIVE

The only way to have a friend is to be one.

I love all 10 quotes in this book, but this is one of my TOP THREE. Why? Because it gets you where you want to be in iife.

I discovered this in 2007, when I began my position as project manager at the headquarter offices in Frankfurt, Germany. My boss put me in charge of the prestigious Nike Manchester United Premier Cup World Finals, a global soccer tournament. After local and nationwide rounds of qualifying on all five continents, only 20 teams met at the annual world finals held in Manchester, United Kingdom, at the training grounds of Manchester United every summer. The players were between 14 and 16 years old and were seen as the next pro generation.

My company had executed this event for several years. The program always consisted of four main components: The opening show including the draw, the tournament itself, the hospitality lounge where the players could eat, rest, and meet, and the final game with the closing ceremony. The final public event was always played at the world famous Old Trafford Stadium in Manchester, one of the most iconic soccer stadiums in the world.

So here I was. It was one of my first and for sure my biggest job as a project manager back then. I was responsible for a six-digit-euro-budget and a crew of almost 100 people over three weeks in Manchester.

I managed to get through the six-month-long pre-production. Luckily my company had done the event in the past, so I pulled helpful information from our archives and from numerous colleagues who were experienced with it. I wasn't shy about asking all kinds of questions internally, so I could shine externally.

Once on site, things got stressful, but we were able to execute as planned. The client was happy, so I was proud even though the rainy weather made the greens super muddy.

The time flew by, and we soon found ourselves preparing to setup for the final at Old Trafford. Two days before the actual event, we were asked to do an in-person meeting with the stadium staff. We presented our 3-D renderings and floor plans for the set-up we had proposed to our client months before.

"There is no way you can do this," was the officials' reaction. "The green is way too wet, and the field boards with the event branding, ceremony stage, and trophy table are way too heavy for the pitch and will definitely destroy the grass!"

My colleagues and I looked at them and pointed to our plans. "But this is what the client wants and expects."

The stadium officials were unwilling to discuss it or compromise because they felt we had never shared these details prior, which was true and our mistake. They thought we were way too late in the game to discuss it.

I responded by telling them that I understood and would accept their decision. Furthermore, I told them that we would go back to the client and inform them first before coming up with a different kind of branding idea which wouldn't include any weights on the grass.

To do so, I asked them if we could go down to the pitch again to be able to come up with an alternative that we could present the client when sharing the bad news with them.

How Being a Friend Made all the Difference

They called the green keeper over the radio and told him to meet us at the players' tunnel.

As we weren't allowed to take any photos, my colleagues worked to capture as many measurements and memories as possible while I chatted with the green keep-er, Tony. He explained his job and that the green was his baby. He described how much work it was to take care of it and that all the rain they had over the last weeks had made it tough.

In turn, I told him about the meeting with the sta-dium official and our current dilemma. I told Tony every-thing: It was my first job, my mistake in not double-check-ing with the stadium, how the client would now be upset, and how tired I felt after almost three weeks of non-stop work.

He smiled at me and said: "You are really pas-sionate about all of this, aren't you? I like that". We exchanged numbers, and I invited him to come over for drinks with the crew that same night. He didn't have time to hang out with us, but I got a text from him later asking for the exact measurements of the field boards again and what the minimum would be to put on the pitch. I could not believe it. After texting back and forth, he told me to check in with him the next day.

We managed expectations with the clients. Of course, they weren't happy about it but understood, and we worked on updating the designs. Call it intuition, but I decided to drive over to the stadium and try to meet with Tony in person again. In traffic it was close to an hour's drive each way, so it was quite a risk that I would just waste time. Something told me to take the chance.

I took a crew shirt from our team and some German beer with me and texted him when I was close to the stadium. I gave him my treats to say thank you for the chat and the extra tour that he'd given us the day before during his lunch break. He asked if I had driven all this way to just say thanks. I let him know we appreciated his help and wanted to make sure we were on his good side while setting up the next day. I told him, "I don't want this to be our last year at Old Trafford."

He smiled and asked me if I had already spoken to the client. I told him that I had, and he replied, "Too bad, because I have decided to make an exception for you. You are so nice and treated me like a friend, like a team player. You respected my job and my perspective, and that's why I want to help you. So, I'll allow a few branding boards and a trophy table on the pitch right after the game for about 30 minutes."

I was speechless. When I recovered from his generous offer, I asked him if I needed something in writing.

His response? "It's all good. We're friends now. I trust you."

When I returned to my colleagues, they were still wrapping their heads around alternatives. After I told them what Tony had offered, they couldn't believe it. They were hesitant about telling the client, but I did so because I knew I could trust Tony.

That said, we set-up the next day, the final was played, the branding was on the boards, and the boards and the trophy table were on the pitch for 30 minutes. Everybody was happy.

We left the stadium exchanging high fives with Tony. A year later, I texted Tony during pre-production. He called me right away just to make sure we would stick with the same set-up and assure him I'd make time to come and see him before the actual event, so we could catch up.

I had made a friend.

The point is that at the end of the day business is about people.

Good People Bring Out the Good in People

It's all about your attitude, your willingness to be friends with people, to respect them, to be kind, and to always make sure you understand their situation. If you treat people you work with like friends, you will have many who will support you and try to get you where you need to go.

For me, this situation was truly meaningful. Being a friend to another changed the approach to get something done. Using the power of friendship and teamwork instead of position or title is stronger, healthier, and most

often the most efficient way to succeed.
So, Remember:

BE KIND.
BE HONEST.
BE TRANSPARENT.
BE RELIABLE.
BE LOYAL.
BE A FRIEND.

Do What You Love
Love what You Do

SIX

Do what you love.
Love what you do.

"Do what you love. Love what you do." These energizing words contain an essential key to success. Living by them enables you to keep up with the pace, stress, and challenges in the business world.

A number of jobs these days require employees to travel. That translates into being gone for weeks, not having weekends from time to time, and being far away from home, family, and friends. When this happens, work feels endless, 24/7, with no time to do anything else.

The only way to not feel lonely, overly exhausted, or longing for a break is to create a niche for yourself where you do what you love and love what you do.

In 2011, I burned out. The first several years of my career, my desire to be the best I could be pushed me to work on as many different accounts as possible to acquire the experience I needed. I did local meetings for a bank in Frankfurt, expo booths for a financial consulting company throughout Germany, a roadshow for an investment company in various German cities, fashion shows for an organic shoe factory in Milan and Berlin, press conferences for the German government in Berlin, electronic music festivals, hospitality lounges during Berlin Fashion week, VIP-automotive incentives in Switzerland, or any kind of internal corporate meeting where technical support and stage build-outs were required.

It exhausted me, and I started complaining about the travel, the clients, and my colleagues. I felt like I wasn't getting paid enough and work had taken over my life.

First, know that I am a sneaker girl. I do love to travel. I am a foodie. I love doing any kind of workout inside or outdoors. I am passionate about details, bright colors, and interior design. Besides that, I love sports and like the team player vibes and the athletic attitude that comes with every sport.

With that said, you can imagine how it felt to me to do a local event for a bank. The dress code, strict Corporate Identity, formal way of communication, and air-conditioned hotel meeting rooms weren't my world at all. I always managed to get through it, but I didn't feel passionate about it and fell out of love with my job. Sure, it sounded fancy when I told my friends what I did, but to me it wasn't at all. I got tired and sick more often than usual.

A new year approached, and I got sick, was in a miserable mood (which is not my nature at all), and decided I needed a break from everything to reconsider my life. It was inconceivable to me that a job and a company that I thought I would love so much wouldn't make me happy anymore.

How to Find What You Love, Do What You Love and Be What You Love

I looked for other jobs and thought of doing something else. But instead of overcomplicating and reconsidering my current job and life, I decided to do the following first:

- write down everything I loved about my job.
- write down everything I hated about my job.
- compare the things I loved with my daily job and job description.
- talk to my boss and explain my situation.

I needed to understand my energy takers and my energy givers.

When I did this, the solution became clear: I told my boss that I need to be fully assigned to the NIKE account.

When I worked on the Nike Account, I got to do

everything I loved. I predominantly worked on their internal sales and global leadership meetings, which took me around the world to: London, Las Vegas, Hawaii, Rio de Janeiro, Hong Kong, Santa Monica, Marrakech, New York, Miami, Tarragona, Rotterdam, and many more wonderful destinations.

We worked with local vendors, so I became acquainted with new people, new cultures, and different work approaches. Because we wanted to create a home away from home for all our guests, we spent a lot of time setting up hospitality lounges. We went shopping for local accessories as well as played around with local styles and kinds of furniture we could afford in the given set-up.

Once an event was over, I always re-arranged my apartment. I adapted what I had learned from various events to my private life. From the flower arrangements to the salad dressings, I always took something "home" for my personal life. I collected tons of collateral from the event itself - business cards, flyers, photos, and giveaways - just all kinds of ideas I liked and found while being gone. Back home I turned them into birthday cards, created artwork, and collected them in a box in my office for the next event or whenever we needed an idea for something similar again.

My associates and I travelled together as a team and worked hard and played hard, and that made us even better. We realized that when we were open to it. we found inspiration everywhere. A wall panel at the restaurant that night could turn into the design inspiration for the stage backdrop the next morning.

We had to test the workouts that we would offer the attendees and created local running maps. We spent hours at night packing for daily room drops where I discovered my passion for beautiful gift wrapping, personal note cards, and just the joy of paying attention to details.

Plus, I was surrounded by all kind of cool sneakers day in and day out.

My point is that my job encompassed all the things I love. These were things that defined me and shaped my character. Today I am a big sneaker head, and I still enjoy what I learned executing Nike events. Because I did what I loved, I didn't get tired of it. The opposite happened. I felt pumped after every event, because I was fueled by the things I love doing.

NOW, Let's Focus on YOU.

Work-Life-Balance is a big phrase these days. Everybody stresses how important it is to have a private life and to make sure not to work too much and not forget to live life to the fullest. Along my journey, I discovered the simple trick to ultimate happiness and unleashing your full potential: doing what you love and loving what you do.

Don't be afraid to marry your private and business

lives. Just make sure they are in a healthy relationship. When starting out, it's often required and normal to work a lot, if you are doing the right thing for YOU. No need to stress. This is just what this chapter of your life is meant to be. Hard work and getting good experience is the pathway to a successful, happy career. Embrace it. If you do, you will notice:

- You start to create your own lifestyle.
- You will be inspired by your work.
- You will be inspired by your private life.
- You will be fueled by the work you do.
- You will find inspiration everywhere.
- You will feel connected.
- You will feel passionate.
- You will feel energized.
- You will be part of a culture.
- You will feel proud of what you do.
- You will be good at what you do because you love what you do.

If you combine your private life with your business life, you will be able to transfer what you see in each world and create the best of both for you personally. For example, a design of the new coffee shop in your neighborhood might be your inspiration for the next hospitality lounge or the kitchen upgrade in your office or even your home.

You never know where life will take you.

That's okay.

Surround yourselves with energy givers, and you will be able to do what you want.

That's for sure.

DO WHAT YOU LOVE. LOVE WHAT YOU DO.

Be
Authentic

SEVEN

Be authentic.

If you want to be successful in today's business world and the digital age, it's more important than ever to be authentic and to have social skills.

What makes a leader authentic? Why is a business person different when authentic and using social skills?

In this chapter I will explain how to be authentic in business. I will share how to use social skills and explain why they will set you apart from the competition.

Let's first start with a bit of my experience.

In 2016, I was an honoree of the "Forty under 40" Award. This award is presented by the *Portland Business Journal*. The jury honors 40 executives under the age of 40 for their excellent business achievements and leadership skills.

Given the facts I had no college degree, had only

been working in the United States for a few years, and was a 31-year-old foreign female, I was extremely surprised and very proud.

During the award ceremony, the committee introduced the honorees and presented their exceptional achievements. They honored me for setting up the first U.S. branch of my German production company and because it had gone from two to 50 employees and achieved significant annual revenue increases in just two years. The jury defined my leadership style as my Number One success factor.

My leadership and business approaches (and the reason for my success) are very simple: BE AUTHENTIC. BE YOU.

I never changed so people would like me. I stayed true to myself and knew that the right people would like me anyway.

If you are authentic, the following can lead you to career success:

BE AUTHENTIC • BE YOU
BE YOU • BE IN YOUR COMFORT ZONE
BE IN YOUR COMFORTZONE • BE ABLE TO LISTEN
BE ABLE TO LISTEN • BE ABLE TO RESPOND
BE ABLE TO RESPOND • BE ABLE TO SERVE OTHERS
BE ABLE TO SERVE OTHERS • BE ABLE TO MAKE
OTHERS SUCCESSFUL
BE ABLE TO MAKE OTHERS SUCCESSFUL •
BE SUCCESSFUL

The above formula illustrates how to create incredible business opportunities. However, there isn't a three-step plan to execute this formula, because everything depends upon an individual's social skills. Unfortunately, classes for social skills are rarely offered in school.

Social Skills and How to Develop Them
I learned social skills from mingling with people — both people my age and those older and younger. From them, I learned to: be a friend, listen to my heart, and say what I mean and mean what I say. I have always handled matters in a personal but professional way which automatically comes across as confident and convincing, because it puts me in my comfort zone. Being in my comfort zone makes me safe and self-confident. It gives me enough energy to focus on new things as well as the people with which I work. This situation enables me to listen to others and to be open to their wishes, needs, and challenges.

Once I understand where they need help and what they really wanted to achieve, I know what to offer them. I then discover my "perfect spot" in our working relationship. Based on that, I can service them accordingly to their needs.

Let me share an example to make this clear. One day I got a call from a new client. He introduced himself and told me he only required three banners. He thought we only needed to define the size. I explained we could produce any size, so he requested prices on three different sizes. I responded I was happy to put the numbers on paper for him, but it wouldn't be practical. I explained, "Imagine you are trying sell a pair of sneakers to a person, and he is only asking you for three different prices. If you know a little bit more about the occasion and circumstances in which the shoes would be used, it would probably be a lot easier, right?" He appeared to get upset. I quickly offered to meet him, whenever it would be convenient for him, to tell me a little bit more about the event and the story behind it. He asked me to meet him over lunch that day to accommodate his busy schedule. I jumped in my car, met him over lunch, and we talked for over two hours. Instead of asking him his requirements, I asked him to tell me about the event and its story first. It turned out that he was working on a huge innovative event series. Two hours later, I had learned about his current job, the pressure that came with it, and the tight schedule he was confronted with to execute the event. The banners were history, and we created an entirely new experience for nim. He was blown away by our service capabilities. The program was a huge success. He got a promotion out of it, and we made a lot more money than just three banners would have been.

Can you see why my social skills are extremely helpful and service-orientated to the prospective client?

Social skills enable a person to be different, personable, and more approachable. They put others at ease. And, in a digital world, social skills create job and success guarantees. Machines react. People with social skills respond appropriately. The most important single ingredient of a formula for success is the knack of getting along with people.

Why You and Your Authenticity Are Irreplaceable

Many people try to replace personal conversations with digital tools these days. Many companies aim to streamline their processes and create pre-defined work flows to be more efficient. In addition, human resource departments have never been bigger, and a lot of corporations believe that they can optimize their potential and talent management by job descriptions and responsibility charts. They try to create human positions which function within the developing software surroundings, almost like little robots.

In the digital future, a robot voice might have taken the order of three banners and would have created an automated, digital response including a quote. At some point, a project manager *might* have gotten involved to talk about the details of the event as well as take care of the actual set-up.

The effort of the project manager would have been minimal. It would not have been a big job, and the performance of the project manager probably would have been measured by the response time, the efficiency, and the final margin. And, probably a few years down the road the company could question the human position completely in this process.

That's why YOU need to use your social skills if you want to achieve more. No matter how good software will be and where the development of robots will take us in a few years, people will always deal with people. People won't disappear. Success will always be achieved by people.

Learning a process or taking another class to perfect sales strategy or becoming an expert for the company's new software will not replace social skills. Not having them will limit your career path. So, whenever you have the chance to work on your social skills, please do so. It is way more important than any other certification. Your social skills make you differ from software, a variety of processes, or any robot. They enable you to respond.

You differ when you:

- learn how to respond authentically, not just react.
- invest a few hours more in the beginning of a working relationship.
- listen to your heart and approach a new job differently than described in your job description if needed.
- make time to meet your clients in person and be an active listener.
- be present, be focused, pay attention to your client's body language.
- put yourself in your client's shoes and take the client's perspective.
- stay on task.
- call people and communicate clearly instead of texting and emailing only.
- remember to be a friend and use their names when speaking to your clients.
- show empathy and encourage the client.
- say what you mean and mean what you say when sharing ideas.
- step out of your box to resolve conflicts.
- celebrate success together.

REMEMBER: People serve people. Treat everyone the way you would like to be treated.

Stop Chasing Perfection and Be Yourself

Let's go back to my experience for a moment.

I was far from perfect. I was quite young given the role and responsibilities I had. I succeeded because I never pretended to be perfect or to be more experienced than others. I did not remain 100 percent professional and 100 percent appropriate in every situation.

Because I was authentic, my team knew when I was in a bad mood and needed support from them. Because I was authentic, I had an opinion. My associates and my clients could tell how passionate I was for every project because I was frustrated when things didn't go right and even happier when everything worked out perfectly. Because I was authentic, I cared about the people on my team and the details of every project. My real character helped me execute my job. Sometimes the tasks were far off the job description I had been given.

And that's the point. The current business world is very structured. HR departments have never been bigger, and a lot of corporations are hoping to optimize their potential and talent management by perfectly defined work flows and job descriptions as well as roles and responsibility charts. One of the goals is to make sure all employees have the chance to perform at their best and their performance can be measured, categorized, acknowledged, and awarded.

That also means assuring you will make a good employee when you stick to all these rules and fulfill all your tasks according to your "to do" list. It won't hurt, and you will be a solid member in any corporate working environment. You will be able to react to the tasks you will be given.

However, if you obey all rules, you will miss all the fun, and if your goal is to achieve more, to get promoted, and become a leader, you must step out of the box to respond and not just react. That means being authentic, saying what you mean, and meaning what you say. Take action where you think it is needed, even if it is not in your job description. Be an active listener and tell your associates and clients what you think if you feel it's important for the success of the project.

People may hear your words, but they feel your attitude.

PAUSE

to balance

EIGHT

Pause to Balance

I have always wondered how great leaders make time to work out, travel for inspiration, spend time with their families, and pursue hobbies while performing demanding jobs. To me, they appear to have a great work-life balance. In interviews, I've heard them admit that they "pause to balance," which is an important piece of their success.

Let me take you through my experience and how I learned what work-life balance really means and why taking a break from time-to-time will make you even more successful.

In 2010, I was the project management team lead at the Berlin branch of my company. I was known to be one of the first people entering the office in the morning and among the last leaving at night. For me, I loved what I did, and my passion for it fueled work on developing a new internal team structure along with numerous other projects.

During the week I had no time to work out, to meet friends, or to take care of any personal responsibilities. I ate out most of the time because I didn't have time to go grocery shopping and cook at home.

I didn't understand how others managed to do all those activities outside of work during the week. My assumption was that they either didn't work as much or as hard as I did or that they held higher positions which allowed them the luxury of a personal assistant. I was completely wrong.

How I learned My Lesson

We were planning a European Sales Conference in Las Vegas. The program included a week-long meeting for over 1,000 attendees who flew in from Europe. We had to set-up over 40 fully-equipped breakout rooms as well as three huge stage sets for fashion and entertainment shows. One of the highlights of the week would include a "5k Elvis Run on the Las Vegas strip". Our goal was to make it into the *Guinness Book of World Records* by creating the largest group of people dressed as Elvis Presley and running on the strip. Besides that, we were asked to plan several themed dinners and a glamourous closing party.

The time difference between Las Vegas, Berlin, and our clients, who were based in Amsterdam, Netherlands, meant long days for us. We communicated with our client during the day and connected with local vendors starting late afternoon through the night if required.

To me, personally, the combination of being responsible for a team of more than 10 project managers and assistants as well as overseeing a European sales meeting was very stressful and extremely challenging. Given that fact, I was convinced I must be super-disciplined and work as much as I possibly could to get as many tasks completed within a day, since new ones would pop up daily.

When I couldn't see a light at the end of the tunnel for weeks, I decided that I needed an assistant or even better, a sister in crime, with whom I could share my work and my brain. After talking to the HR department and my bosses, the frustrating answer was they couldn't approve and afford an additional employee at that time. They did support the idea to find a freelance worker to jump in and help me out.

Hiring a freelancer sounded like a great solution, but I didn't have the time to interview people and wasn't sure if I had enough money in my event budget to afford somebody. Additionally, it didn't seem efficient to me to onboard a freelancer to only assist with one project. I had a million reasons why this wasn't the right solution for me at the time. Although I wanted help, every proposed solution felt too complicated to me.

So, here I was. I had a ton of work to do, and the

event required my undivided attention. We barely could fulfill all the client's needs and take care of all requests, even though we worked constantly. We did the best we could every day, and the client was appreciative. But we were reacting and not acting. I frequently grew frustrated but tried to be strong and professional by doing whatever it took to make the client happy.

Signs That Will Indicate It Is Time to Take a Break
After one very long day, I considered:

- I was in doubt. I was in doubt about the event, the process, my job, my life. Just everything.
- The more I worked the more work occurred. I felt like I was in a devil's circle.
- I was tired and unmotivated. My brain was fried.
- I felt unsuccessful, unaccomplished, and inefficient.

The following day I wrote an email to my team explaining I would stay home for the day. I wasn't sick; I needed a break.

At some point, I got up and went for a long walk. I stopped at a coffee shop. I sat down with my coffee and didn't check my phone which was out of character for me. I just stared out of the window. I saw people out for a run, moms walking their children, and friends chatting with each other. The event in Las Vegas seemed far away and did not exist in the world I observed. In that moment, I realized that working isn't the whole of life, only part of it. If I only worked, I'd miss out on the other part of life. The fun part of it.

That same day, I met with a good friend. Five minutes into our conversation, she said: "I think you need a sister in crime or an assistant. That should be your priority now". She was right, and I was happy that she re-confirmed what I had recognized a few weeks earlier.

The day passed, and at the end of it I felt better. During that time, I:

- went for a run
- did some retail therapy
- cooked a meal
- met a friend
- took care of my laundry
- colored in my coloring book
- took a nap
- chilled on my couch and spend some time in my apartment

Long story short, I did things that brought me joy.

I went to bed feeling happy and excited about the next work day and all the things that I needed and *wanted* to tackle. I spent the day *refueling and re-energizing.* In that one day, I felt the amount of work I faced was achievable again.

Taking a break enabled me to:

- remember my life was good and I really liked my job.
- decide to be happy again and to approach challenges with a positive mindset.
- be mindful and take care of myself.
- learn to say no and be okay with it.
- set my priorities.

The next morning, I posted this question on my private Facebook account: "Who has time the next three months and wants to work in the event industry?"

When I arrived at the office, my boss asked if I had lost my mind in the last 24 hours, because he had seen the post. He couldn't imagine that I would find a serious candidate that way.

"Let's wait and see," I said, "and if I don't find anybody, it was an easy, budget-friendly, and not time-consuming try. Don't worry!"

I could tell he was perplexed by my optimism and positivity, so he just smiled and nodded.

Believe it or not, a few hours later I received a text from a girl I had met during an event set-up earlier that

summer at the Nike store in Berlin. She had been an interr
at Nike at that time, and we happened to connect on
Facebook. During the two weeks that we had executea a
press conference each morning before the store openea,
the two of us had gotten along very well.

We met at the office the next day, and before I
knew it I had the best assistant I could have dreamed of
for the next three months and beyond. We came to a very
fair agreement, and she knew that she could be offerea
a permanent job after the first three months. My fears of
endless time spend on onboarding were gone. I realized
that if you are open for help and you hire the right person, it creates immediate stress release and support.

Ways to Find Your Work-Life Balance

Based on my experience the day before, we decided to
work and live by the principal of "pause to balance" as
of day one. This kind of work-life balance didn't mean to
work less and live more. It also didn't mean to work on a
strict nine-to-five schedule. We did make things happen.
Our job was to get the events done, to make the clients
shine, and to ensure that our team was happy. And sometimes that meant long days, overtime, and the odd week-
end here and there.

Nonetheless we took care of our needs.

Sometimes that meant:

- *yoga*
- *coffee*
- *yoga and coffee*
- *cocktails after work*
- *a day off*
- *seeing the family*
- *playing with the dog*
- *taking a nap*
- *shopping*
- *arts and craft*
- *going on a run*

No Secret formulas, self-help books, or perfect company for which to work exist to give you a balanced life. It takes work, and a lot of it is simply analyzing your needs and those of the people you love to achieve a balance that works for you.

In reality, your idea of balance can be whatever you want it to be. Here is what I do to create balance in my life on a regular basis:

- I take care of myself. I try to rest, exercise, and eat properly.
- I have priorities. Balance does not mean cramming in every activity possible. Less is more. Focus on what is important to you depending on your stage in life.
- Try to be efficient. I always sit down at the

beginning of the week and plan and put things on schedule; both work and private appointments.

- Embrace the unexpected. I go with the flow. My plan and my schedule always change, but that's okay. I do what it takes to get the things done that pop up, and then try to get back to normal.
- Always try to stay positive. A negative mind will never create a positive life. I try to stay positive and optimistic.

By sticking to these simple tricks, my sister in crime and I managed to accomplish the tasks we were given in 2010, and the Elvis Run made it into the *Guinness Book of World Records*.

By the way, seven years later, when I left my position in Portland, Nancy, the girl I found on Facebook who became my sister in crime, was promoted to replace me. So, as you can see, that "pause to balance" was what made us both successful and helped us to create happy, healthy lives for ourselves.

If you feel too busy, take a break.

Never forget to have fun.

PAUSE TO BALANCE.

life starts
at the end
of your
comfort zone

NINE

*life starts at the end
of your comfort zone.*

Every successful person will agree with this quote.

This chapter is about its meaning and how to determine if and where you are in your comfort zone. I discovered the end of mine in the summer of 2016.

I had been in my position in Portland for four years. During that time, the company grew from two to over 50 employees. We shed our German newbie title and emerged as a well-established event provider in the U.S. Our numbers were stellar. Being chosen as Nike's preferred partner for the Olympic Games in Rio de Janeiro, Brazil, was icing on the cake for us.

Our main job was to set up athlete hospitality. In addition to this extraordinary and massive project, we were asked to execute a huge brand experience during the USTF National Track & Field Championships, which also served as the qualification track meet for the Olympics, in Eugene, Oregon.

Life is Great in the Comfort Zone

My childhood dream, to be part of the Olympics in some way, had been realized. I loved my job and my life. Nothing could stop me.

I was clearly in my comfort zone because:

- I loved my job and its challenges.
- Although it was challenging I felt I had things under control.
- My desire to succeed was bigger than my fear of failure.
- I knew and I had confirmation that we were successful.
- I had found my purpose.
- I was happy with my private life.

The experiences we created for the Olympics-related events were extremely successful, and we were proud, happy, and exhausted in the end. The memories, like the unbelievable heavy tropical rain, the visa challenges we overcame, the colorful street art, the yellows and greens of the beaches, the kindness and happiness of our Brazilian hosts, and the sporting events we attended will last a lifetime.

Once the games were over and the crew was back

home after several months, i took time off. My body was tired, and my brain was empty. I went on vacation and didn't really do anything, which is very untypical for me. Back in the office after a few weeks, I expected to be re-charged and energized again. Surprisingly, although my body felt rested, my brain wasn't at all.

I lacked the ability to light that inner fire to carry on and fuel me with energy, motivation, and the business hunger for which I was known.

My bosses and co-workers didn't notice. They hoped slower days would allow me to embrace the eas-iness that I could have enjoyed during those days. They wanted me to pick the cherries of the hard work I had put in for more than a decade and promised to work with me on new goals which would once again challenge and motivate me.

However, I realized that the wind of change was blowing in my direction and that I had probably reached the end of my comfort zone. I recognized this, because:

- My work did not inspire me anymore.
- I felt bored by my daily tasks and challeng-es.
- I couldn't think of another job within the com-pany that I really wanted to do.
- I was in a terrible mood and miserable and negative, which isn't my attitude at all.

- I felt I wasn't moving forward anymore. I had done the same thing for almost 14 years.
- I felt like people had overtaken me. My comfort zone had come to a standstill.
- I nad a sense I would be moving backwara in my life and career.

Don't Fear Change at the End of Your Comfort Zone

It took me a while to realize that it wasn't the company's fault and didn't have anything to do with my job. It was just me. I was ready for a change. I didn't do what I loved anymore.

I filled my days with endless busy work, not stopping to think about where my life was going. Everyday routine and obligations stagnated my life and blocked my dreams for even more success. Disappointingly, I realized my days were less about what I wanted to do and more about what I felt "I had" to do. I knew I deserved better.

I needed:

- a *life-style* change
- a bold change
- a real challenge

But what did that mean? What could it be? It coulu have been:

- a different position at the same company.
- a new personal goal.
- a change in a relationship or living situation.
- a new hobby.
- the same position at a different company.
- a simple change of attitude.

I honestly didn't know but understood I wasn't happy anymore and needed time to think through the possibilities and challenges for change. It became apparent that I needed to quit my job to make room for time to think without the daily routine of work.

Since I knew that quitting my job would change my life (which is what I wanted), I did it. I changed my life before my life changed me.

Having no idea what to do next clearly took me out of my comfort zone. I worried about money and had to structure my day by myself instead of having a schedule determined by meetings and an office to-do list. Other people didn't dictate my life. I was the only one who could make me get up and figure out what I needed to do.

My last day at work was January, 2017. Since then I had a baby, wrote this book, supported a startup business, received job offers, created dozens of new ideas, and bought another venture. I consulted for a few individuals and volunteered at several organizations. I have been able to spend more time with family and friends than ever before, enjoy a vacation, and pursue my hobbies and new experiences.

After beginning my new life, I realized that starting over is the beautiful moment when you redefine yourself and your purpose. It's become clear what people mean when they say, "Change is good" and "Life starts at the end of your comfort zone."

That's my story, and I couldn't be happier.

I encourage you to always challenge the status quo, take the next step, and make a bold change when life nudges you in a new direction. You decide what that change will be. I promise you won't regret it at all. It just gets better and better.

Remember, life starts at the end of your comfort zone.

TEN

Go. See. Do.

This chapter culminates this book. GO.SEE.DO is my personal key to success, my take-away of my event industry experience, and the maxim by which I live.

While the other chapters contain specific lessons learned in my life, GO.SEE.DO has become my mantra and has helped me master every situation in my past and present. These words will carry me through my future. GO.SEE.DO contributed to my success and happiness. You see, it was hard work to get where I am today. And, the power of GO.SEE.DO has covered every aspect of my business and private life.

Working hard meant I had to make it or break it, take now or never chances, begin anywhere, and be so good they couldn't ignore me. But, I had to combine the hard, disciplined work with real fun, like travel, pausing and balancing instead of paying too much money for seminars or getting additional degrees to find success and happiness.

All of us are surrounded by numerous services and tools that are supposed to make us happy and successful. They lure people to "invest" money for self-improvement. They include business coaches, very expensive private schools, and millions of self-care businesses to feel good, such as massages, pedicures, and fancy gyms. In addition we are told endless variations of status symbols will illustrate our success and happiness.

I am convinced that we don't need any of the above when we stick to the simple maxim: GO.SEE.DO:

When I GO	When I SEE	When I DO
• I move	• I understand	• I try
• I am active	• I focus	• I make it
• I don't stop	• I learn	• I fail
• I experience	• I get inspired	• I learn
• I DO	• I GO	• I GO
• I SEE	• I DO	• I SEE

Each of the listed activities can stand alone but mixed together they provide an outstanding outcome. All are interconnected and a result of each other. When one is initiated, the others will happen automatically.

They are beautiful because all actions and resulting outcomes are priceless. Investing in self, success, and happiness does not have to be expensive, which means it can be accessible to anyone open to it.

That said, I have never spent money on status symbols and expensive business seminars. Rather, I travelled.

Living abroad has shaped me more than I could ever imagine. Every vacation I have taken over the years has proven to me that GO.SEE.DO is the best tool to fix issues that arise during a busy and demanding professiona and private life.

For example:

In December 2015, a friend asked me to go on a 10-day trip to Australia with her the following month to watch the Australian Open. At that time, I hadn't been gone from the office longer than a week and never that far way. The moment she invited me I knew it would be a *now or never* opportunity. I had never been to Australia; we had a place to stay for free in Melbourne; and we had tickets to the Australian Open and enough frequent travel miles to afford the flight.

That said, I agreed to join her on this trip, and we booked the flights.

The week before we were going to leave was one of the worst ever in my job, and I had no idea how in the world I would be able to leave a few days later. We were super busy and went through a corporate HR re-organization which affected every employee working at the company back then. To me it was the worst time to leave, because I didn't want my team to think I would leave them behind or travel on purpose so that I wouldn't have to answer numerous questions; something I never would have done.

My sister-in-crime, Nancy, insisted that I take that trip. She knew that it was time for me to *pause and balance* as the weeks before had been super intense.

It took me out of my comfort zone to leave my folks at the office, my laptop, and my work life behind for ten days. However, the moment the plane touched the ground in Melbourne, I realized again that *life starts at the end of your comfort zone.*

We had the best time ever in Australia. When I travelled, this happened:

- I did **GO**. I moved. I was active.
- I did **SEE:** new people, new places, new cultures, new lifestyles, new worlds.
- I mixed with people, and I learned that *you must be a friend to have a friend.*
- It made me realize and understand who I am, where I come from, who I like to be, and what I like to **DO**. It made me *be authentic.*
- I got inspired.
- I learned.
- I refueled.
- I came back a better version of myself.

When I returned to the office after 10 days of sunshine. tennis, beach, sight-seeing and nothing but good times, I was so energized and motivated *to do what I love and love what I do* again. The time-out in Australia unleashed untapped potential in me so that I could master the challenges we had, and *I could be so good, they couldn't ignore me.*

This trip inspired me so much and revealed again how blessed we are to live in this wonderful world and how many opportunities we all must GO.*SEE*.DO if we are open to it.

I didn't learn GO.*SEE*.DO in school. It is not something that can be taught from one day to the other. It is a never-ending process and a journey that is different for everyone. I can't tell you what will work best for you but want to share a few inspirations that have helped me:

GO TRAVEL:

- Take day trips.
- Be a tourist in your own city.
- Go grocery shopping in a different super market.
- Take city trips.
- Move, move, move. The only bad workout is the one you didn't do. Move your body, and your mind will follow.
- Don't travel with too much of a plan. Let your mind explore. Let Go.

SEE:

- Make time to see.
- Enjoy time offline. Have dinners and spend time with friends and don't bring your phone.
- Don't be a stranger; be a friend.
- Be present.
- Pause to balance.
- Be mindful.
- Give your brain, body, and mind time to process.

DO:

- Make it or break it.
- Be so good they can't ignore you.
- Do what you love. Love what you do.
- Challenge the status quo.
- Say what you mean; mean what you say.
- Try it out.
- Make mistakes.
- Enjoy the ride.

So, please remember that wherever you are in your life and in your career, you are only defined by the walls around you. Everything is possible if you stick to the 10 quotes in this book and you just GO.*SEE.DO.*

Enjoy!
maika

ACKNOWLEDGMENTS

A big thank you and sincere gratitude to all the people that helped me realize my dream to make this book reality. Thanks for your support, encouragement, advice, and love.

Special thanks to:

My husband, Venne, for his endless love, support, and belief in me.

My family and friends (you know who you are) for their greatness, inspiration, patience, love, advice, and help on every level. I can't imagine a life without you all.

Big Thanks to satis&fy (www.satis-fy.com) for being one of the best employers I can think of for young professionals.

To Carol, Andrea, and Anna for helping me to turn my thoughts and quotes into a book. You ladies have been my partners in crime from start to finish and worked tirelessly with me to get it done.

And last but not least, thanks to all young professionals out there. Thank you for taking over and making this world an even better place for all of us.

Maika

ABOUT THE AUTHOR

Maika Janat is a Portland-based creative and event management professional by way of Frankfurt and Berlin, Germany.

Maika worked for a well-respected event production company for 13 years and grew as an intern and producer in Frankfurt to become the U.S. branch president of satis&fy in Portland, Oregon. After running the company's U.S. interest in Portland for just two years, she was honored by the *Portland Business Journal* as one of its *40under40* awardee at the age of 31.

Maika has taken a break from the event world to write this book, give birth to her wonderful daughter, Lucy, and add to her massive sneaker collection gathered from around the globe!

This book summarizes her event career in a practical sense, delving into her real-life experiences, her inspiration, and her motivation. Maika is a true testament to the fact that hard work, commitment, authenticity, and a "go. see. do." attitude are key ingredients to success.

ABOUT THE ILLUSTRATOR

Annalina Väth is a professional visual merchandiser and self-taught artist and calligrapher. Besides her incredible value as a trainee for satis&fy, AG based in Frankfurt, Germany, she was ranked No.3 at the *German Visual Merchandising Championships in 2017* at the age of 21.

Her learning by doing attitude has been the key to turning her passion for calligraphy and hand lettering into a business. Her client portfolio consists of local restaurants, coffee shops, high-end weddings, and a variety of personal stationary requests.

Fueled by her motto, Go. See. Do, her creativity has been inspired by travelling to 24 countries around the world. When she is home, she loves spending time with her family and describes herself as a food lover and sneaker addict.

ABOUT THE BOOK DESIGNER

Kaitlynn Jolley, a 22-year-old graphic designer, has always been strongly drawn to all forms of art and graphic design. An advocate of Go. See. Do, Kaitlynn loves learning new things and embraces everything that allows her to express her creativity.

Like Maika, her inspiration comes from her experiences with people, travel, and new destinations. Kaitlynn recently moved to South Carolina. In her free time, in addition to travel, she reads, draws, and spends time with her two cats, Kovu and Ellie.

listen to your heart

make it
or
break it

now or never

be so
GOOD
they can't ignore you

the only way
to have a friend
IS TO BE ONE

Do What You Love
Love what You Do

Be Authentic

PAUSE
to balance

life starts
at the end
of your
comfort zone

Go.
See.
Do.

Go. See. Do.
Quotes on Postcards

Annalina has created a postcard for each quote contained in this book. Each can be used as a personal reminder on your desk, your refrigerator, or any other place that works best for you. I encourage you to write personal notes for others on them to inspire, to say thank you, or to pay it forward. Believe me; a personal note has magical skills. In our digital world, it will make you different and so good that they can't ignore you.

You can order these beautiful keepsake postcards from
www.mjvonline.com
@mjvonline

... go, see, do ...